Copyright

Keep Calm And Color On ...

Coloring Book

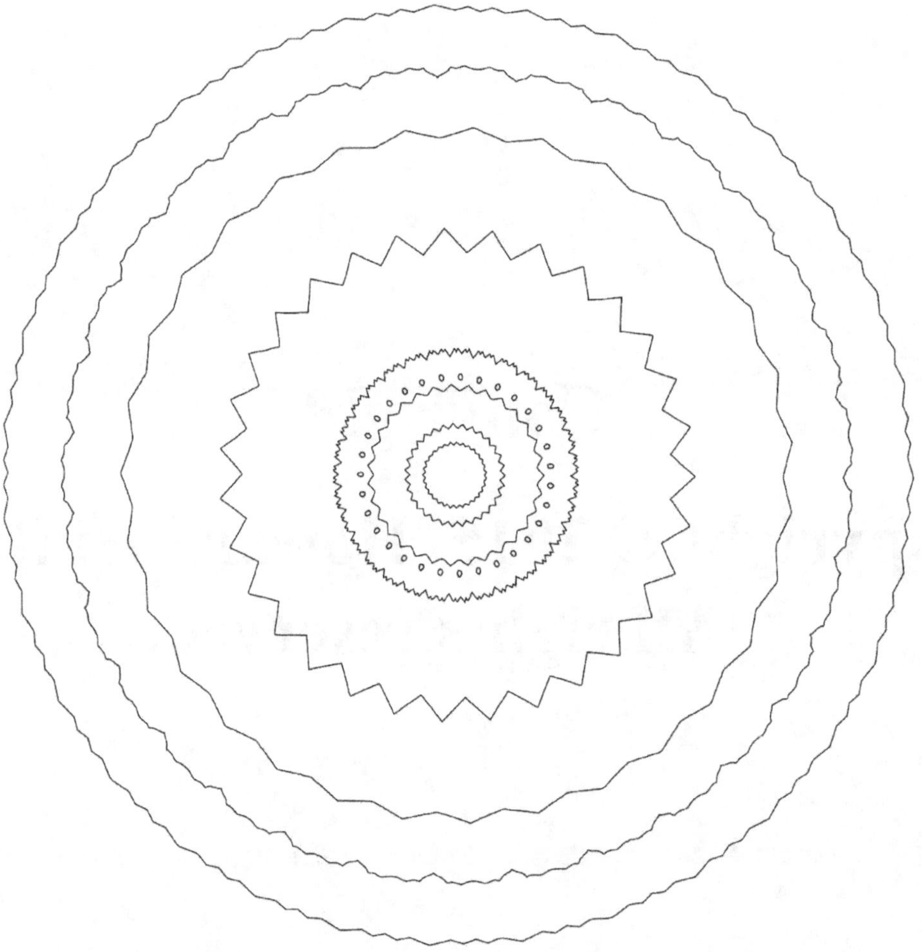

Howard Hinton Jr
Reminders Plus Photography LLC

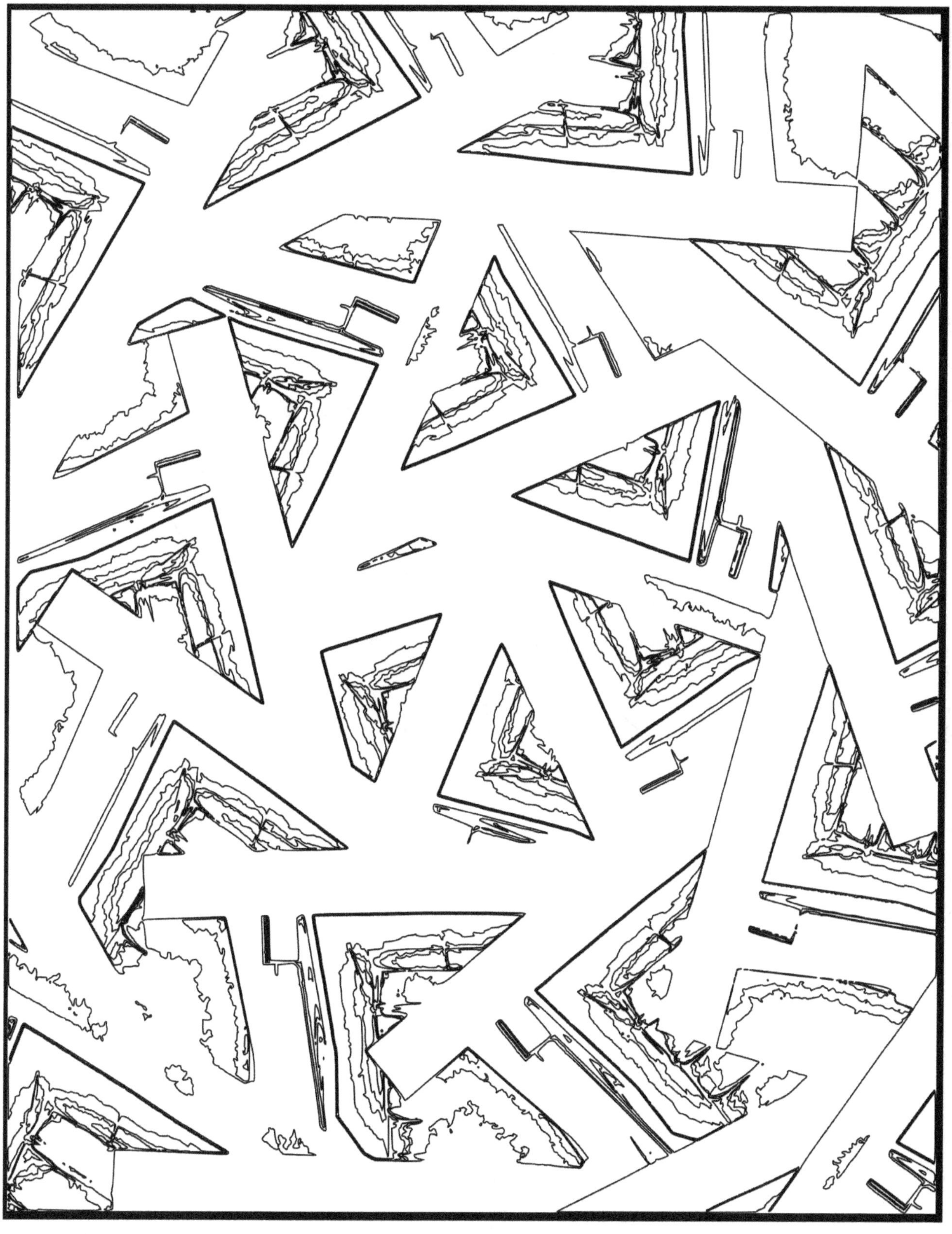

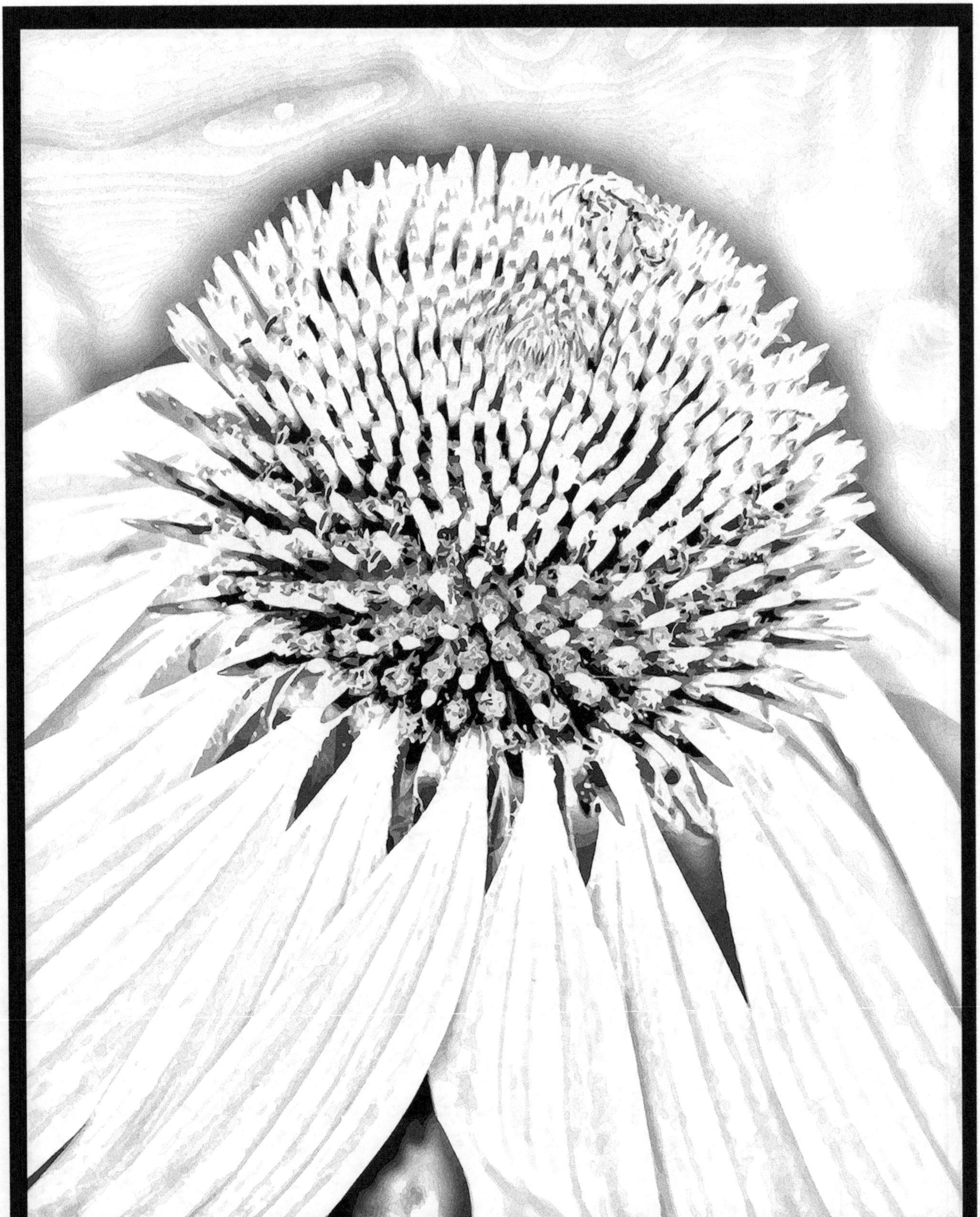

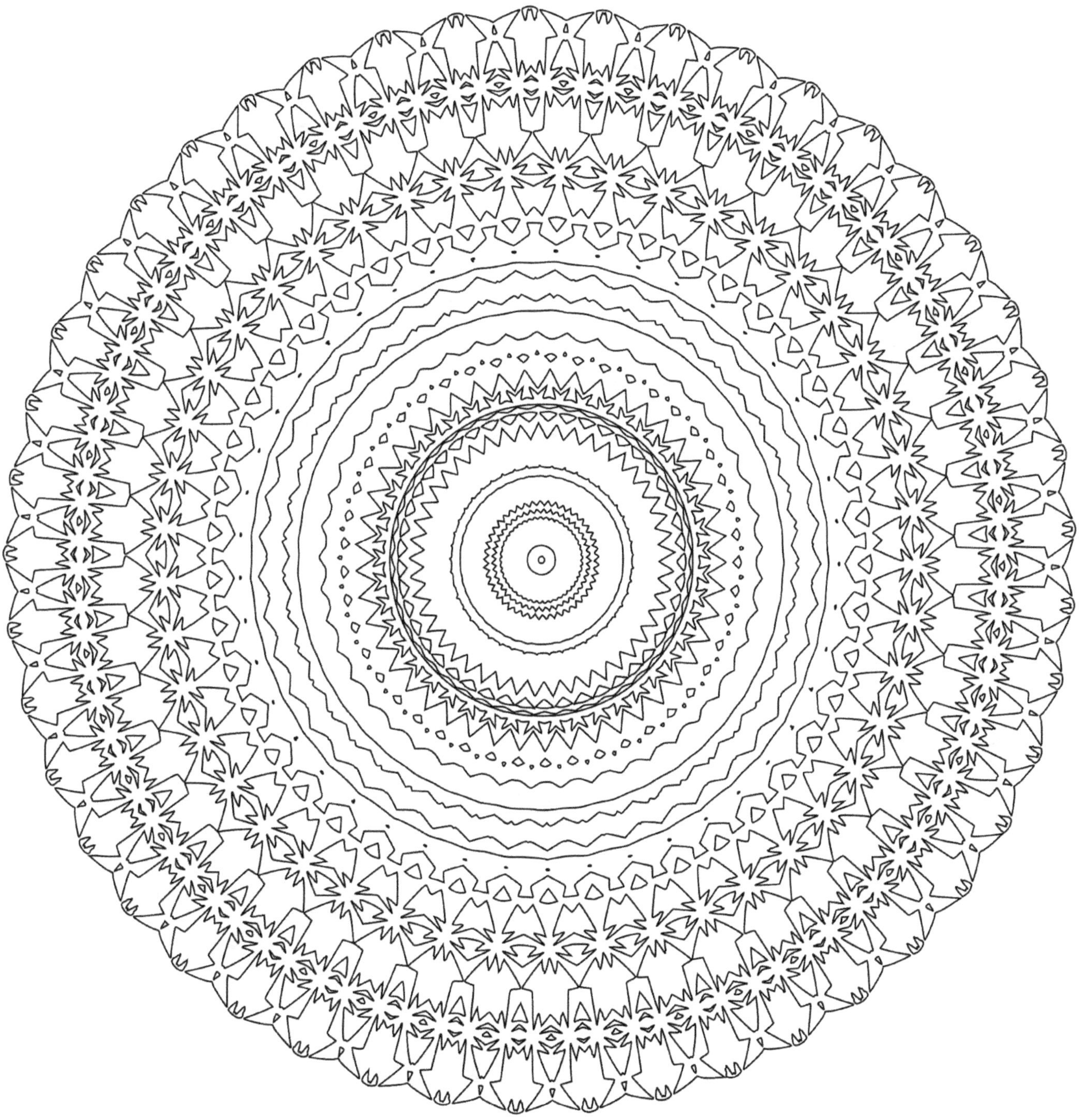

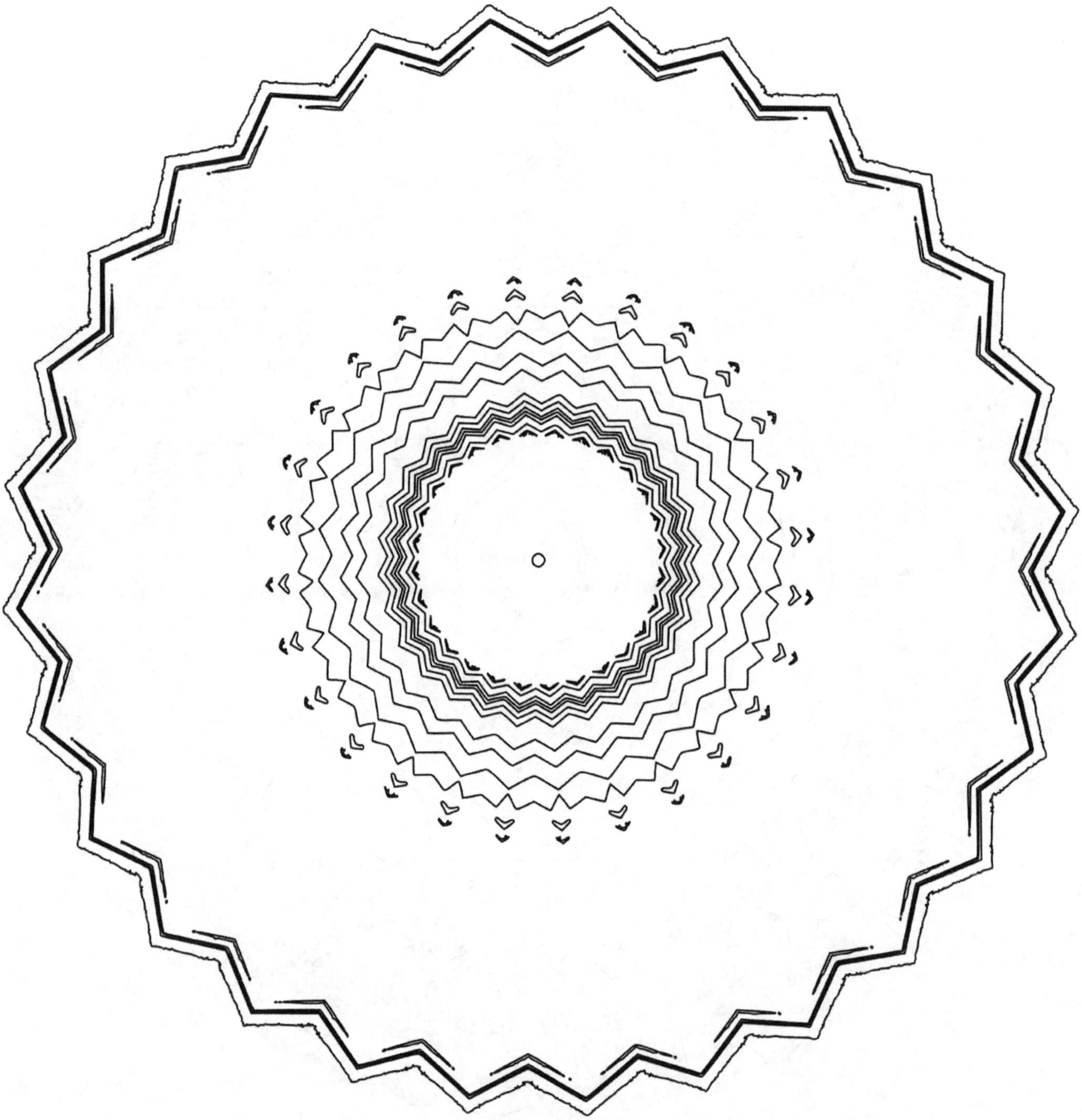

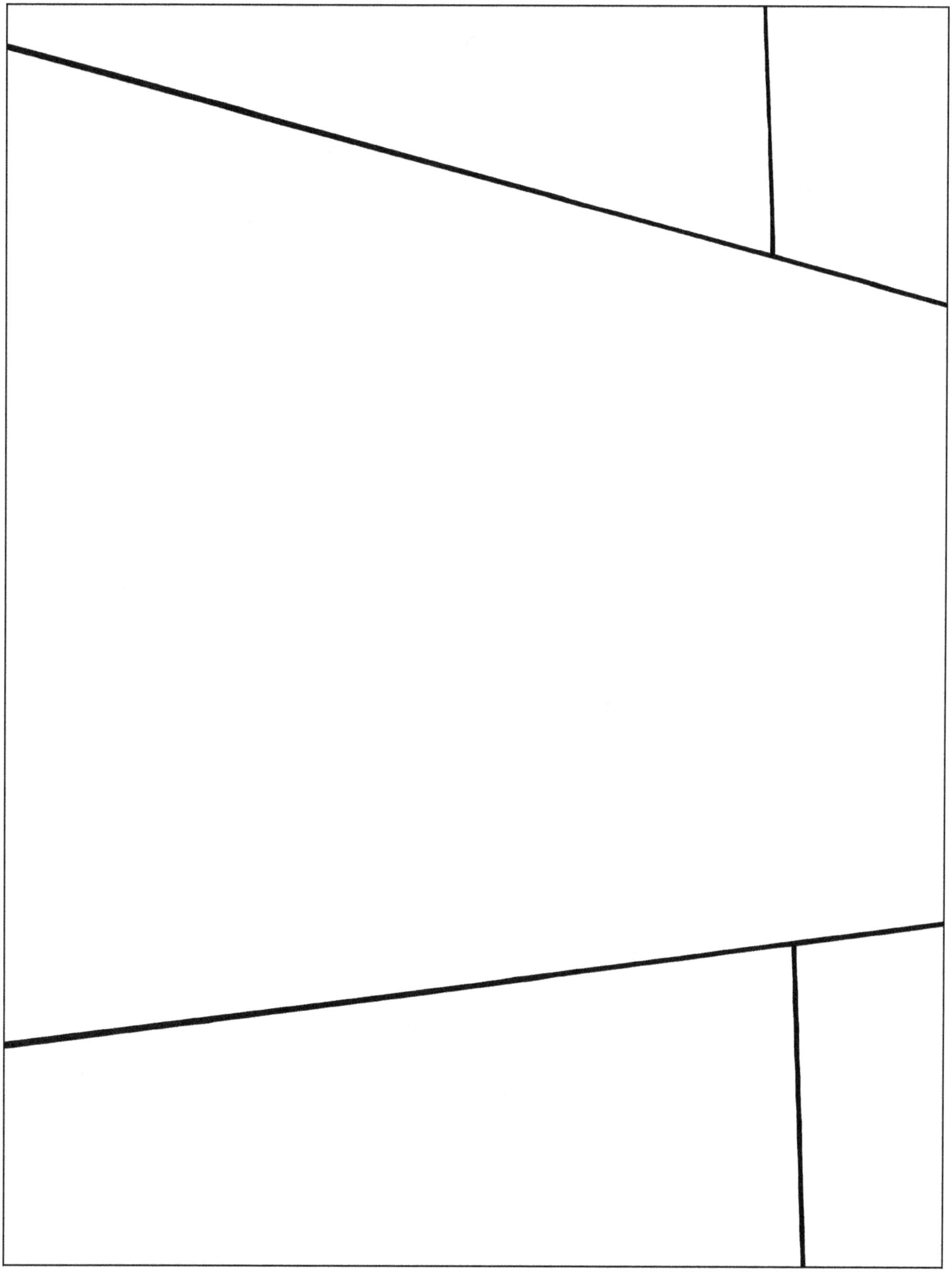

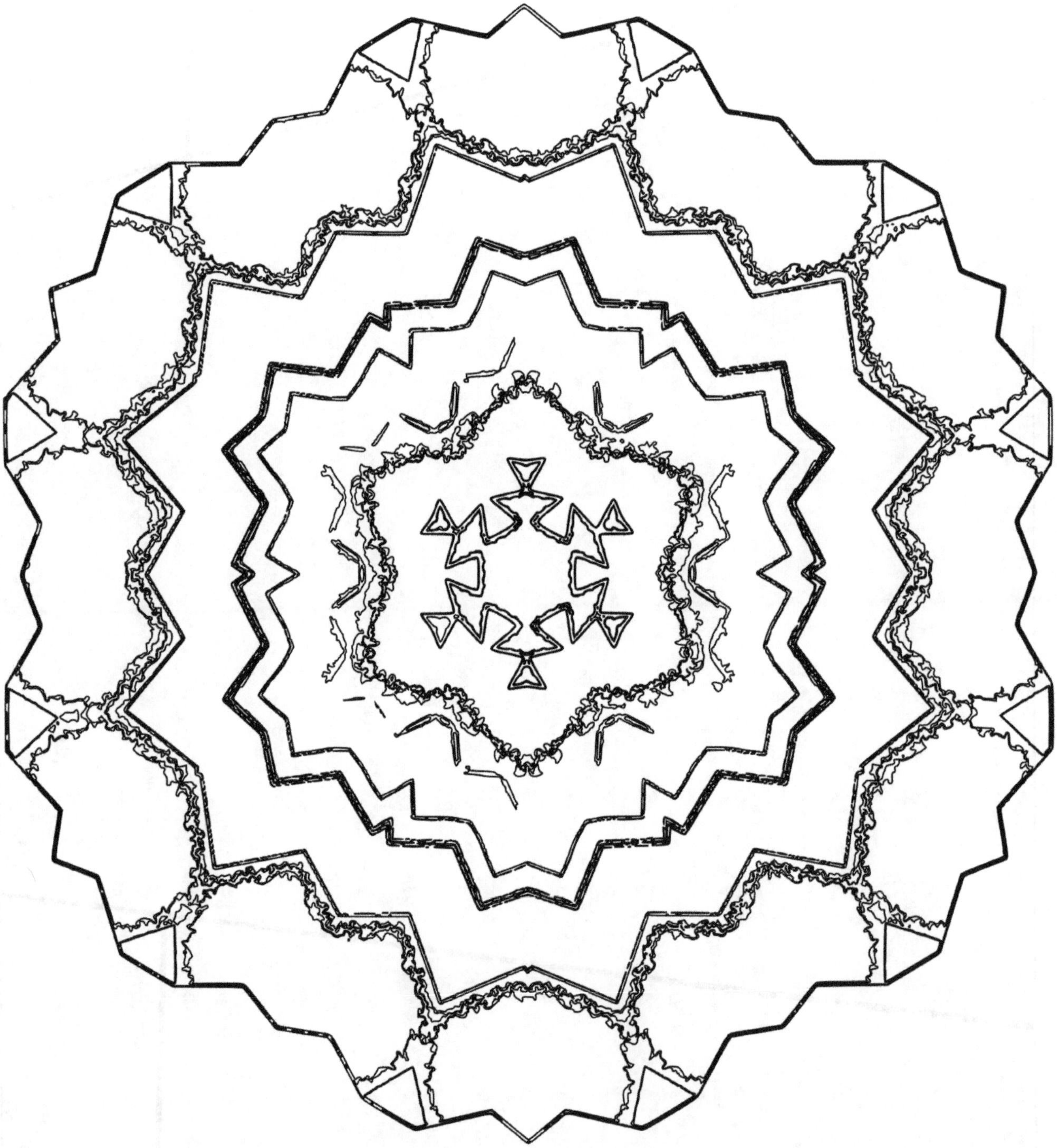

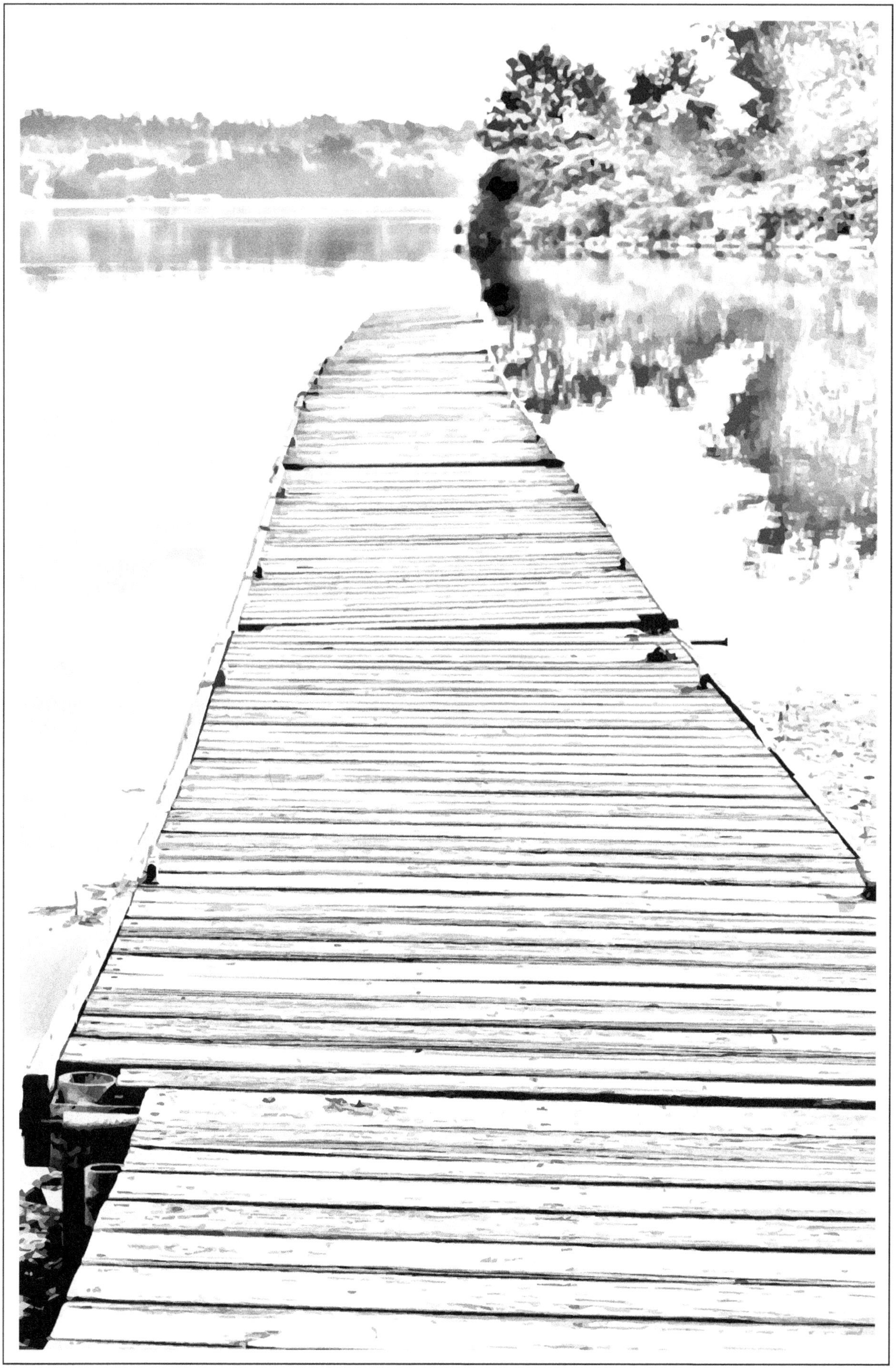

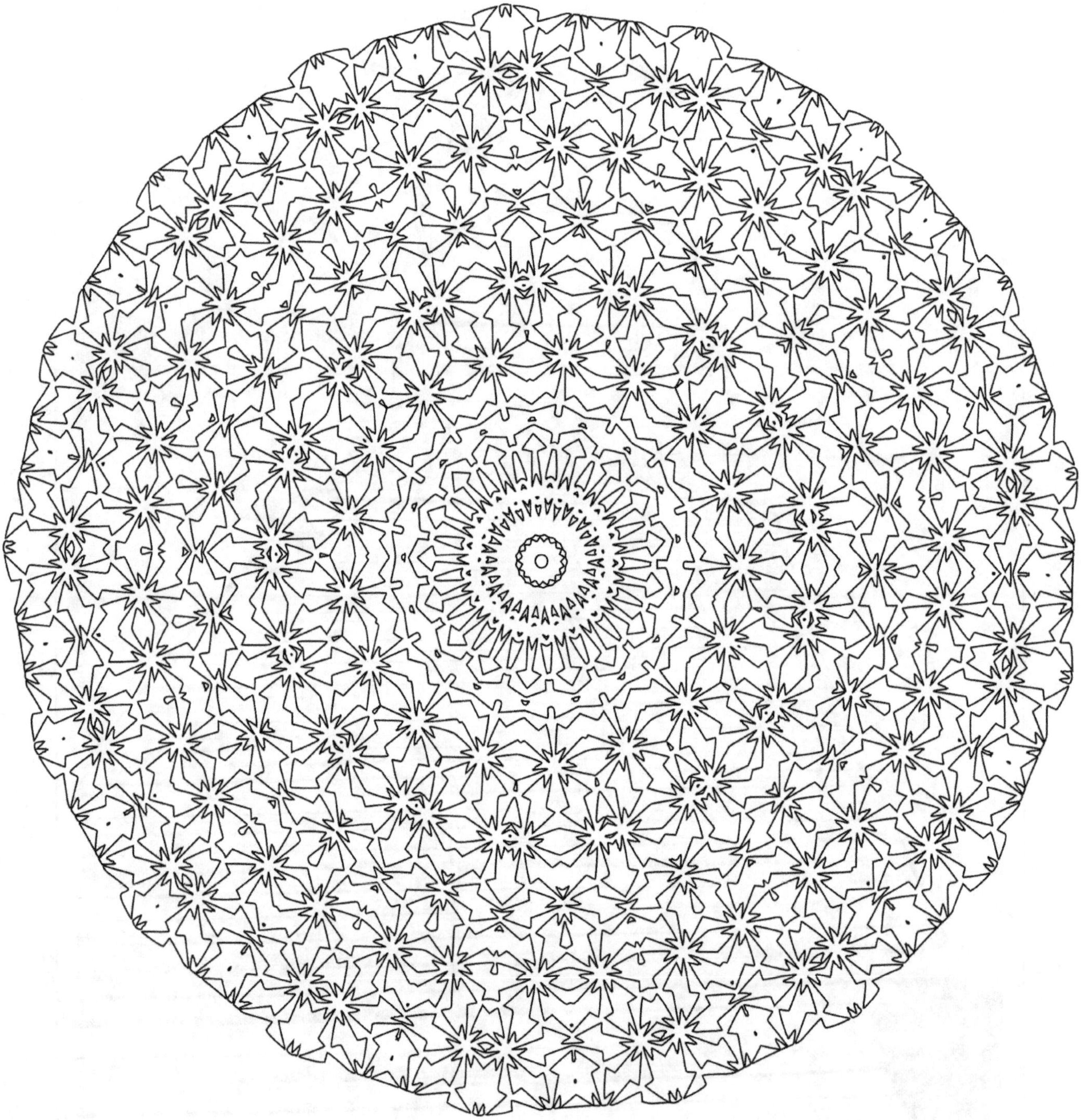

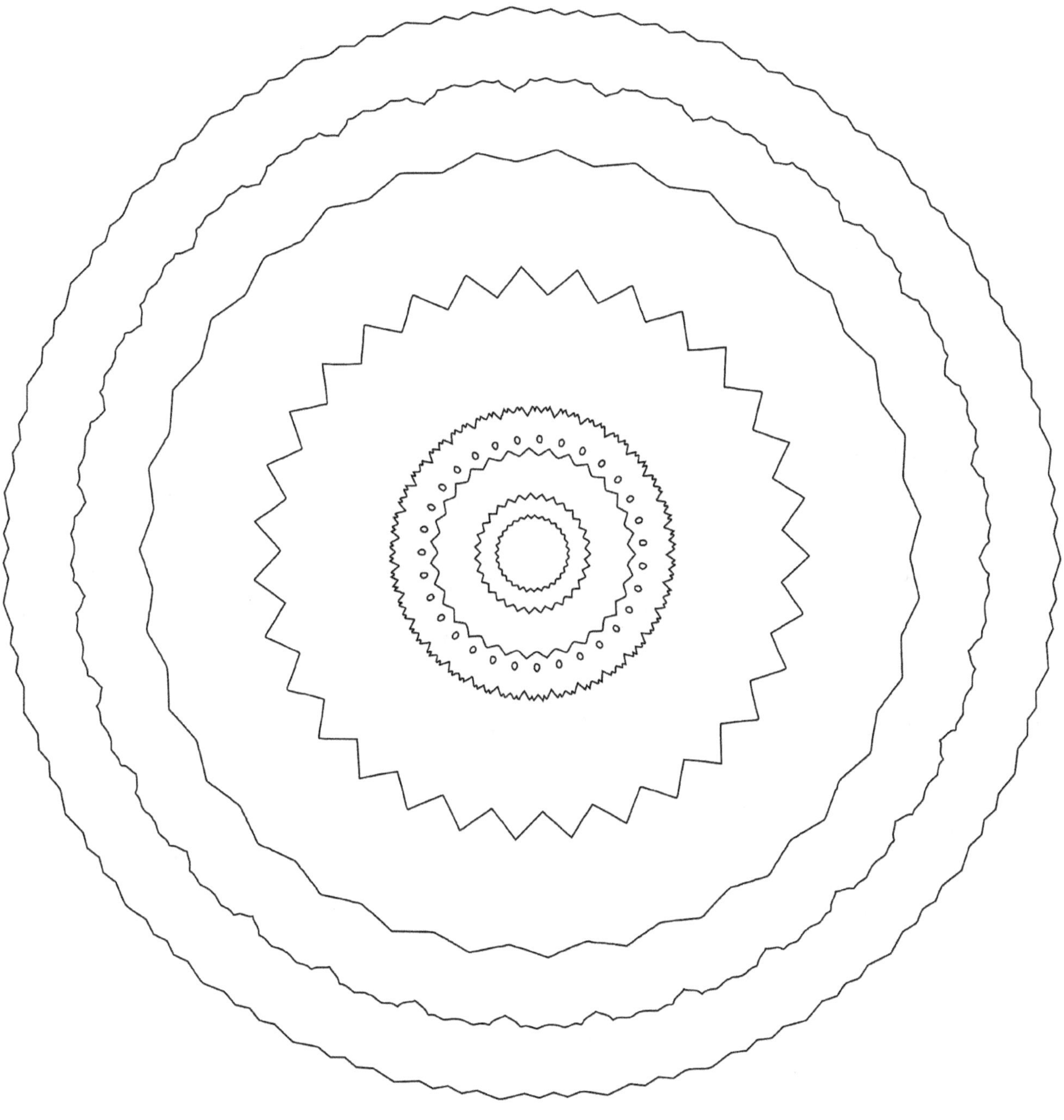

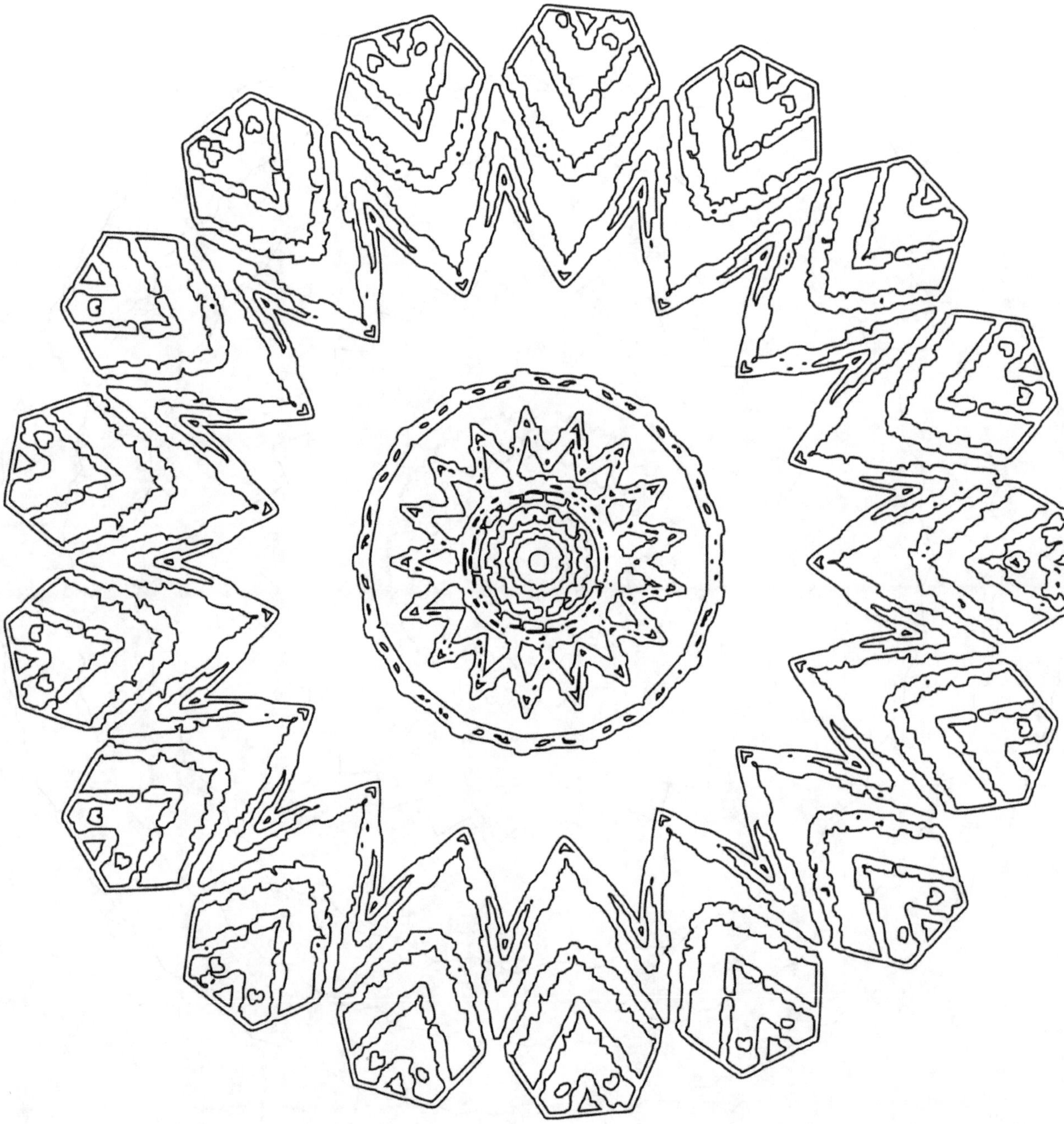

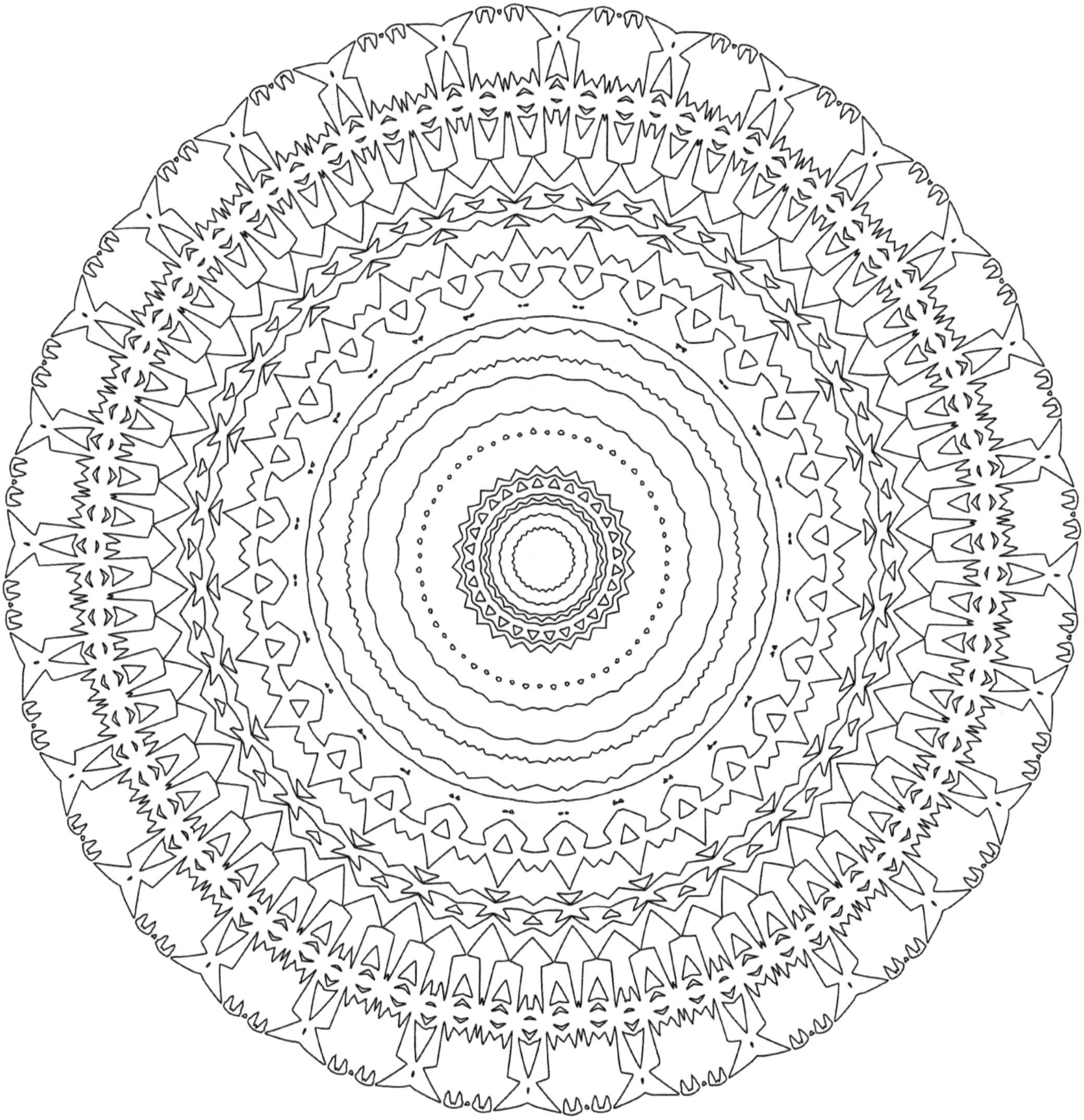

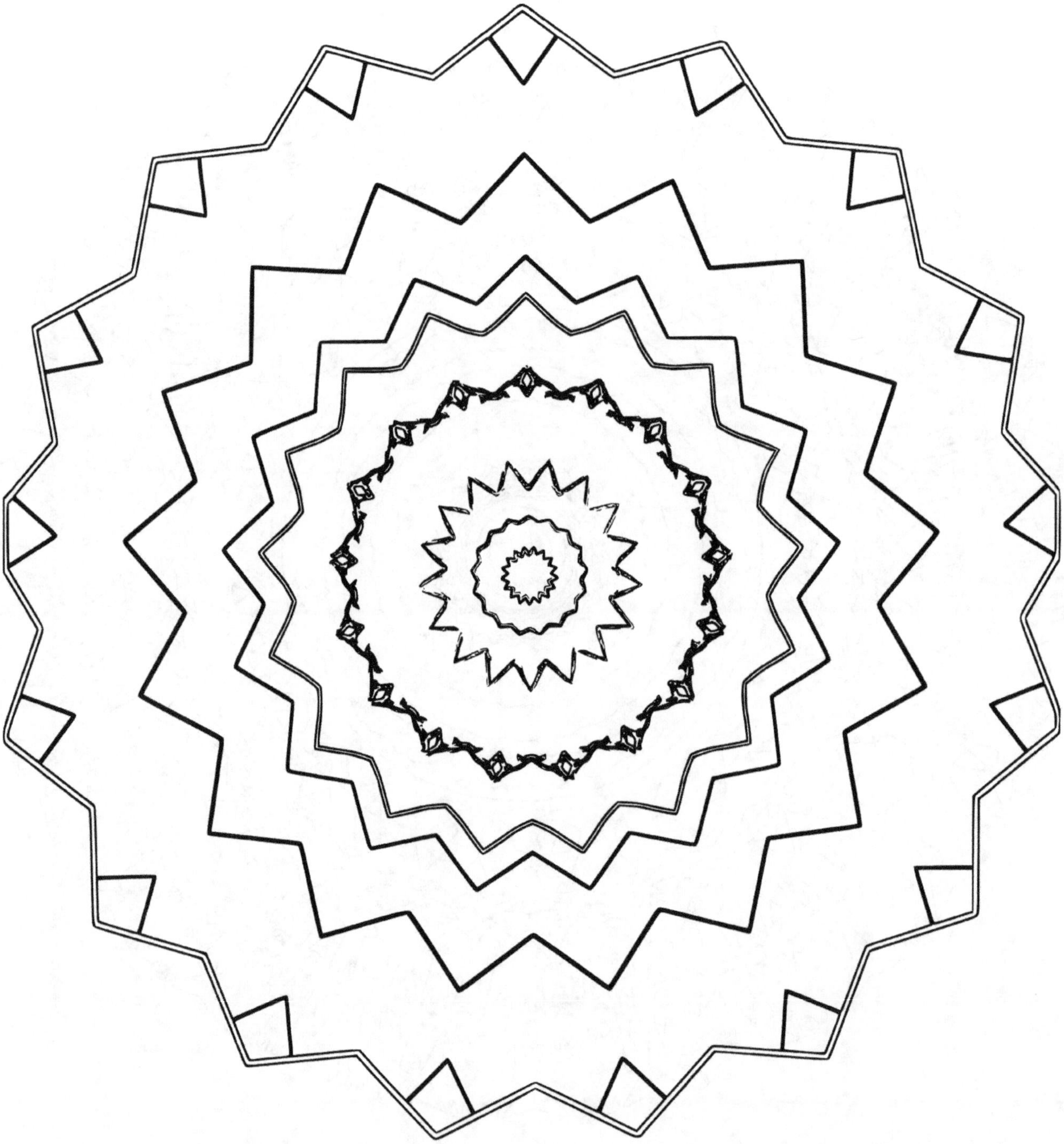

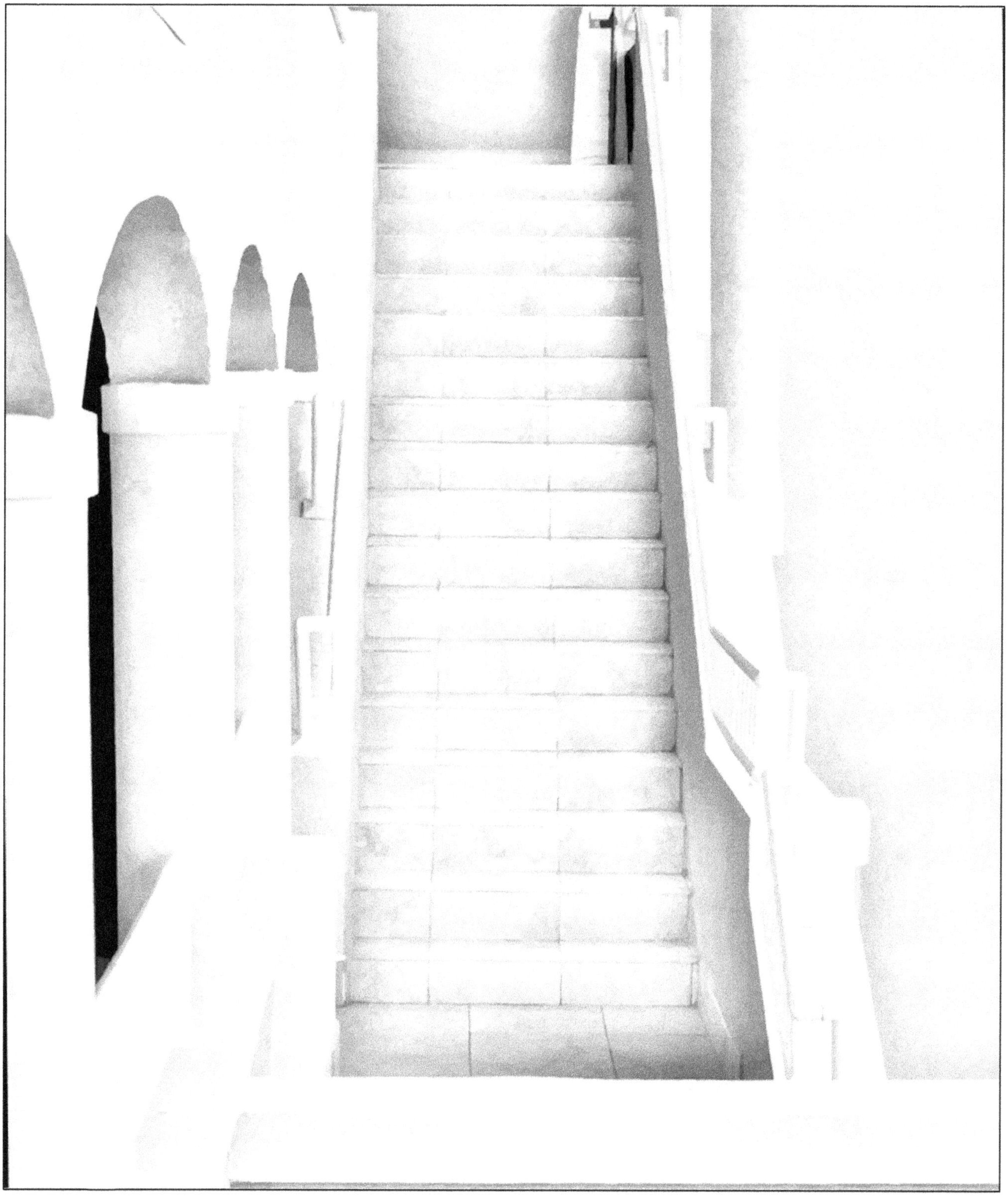

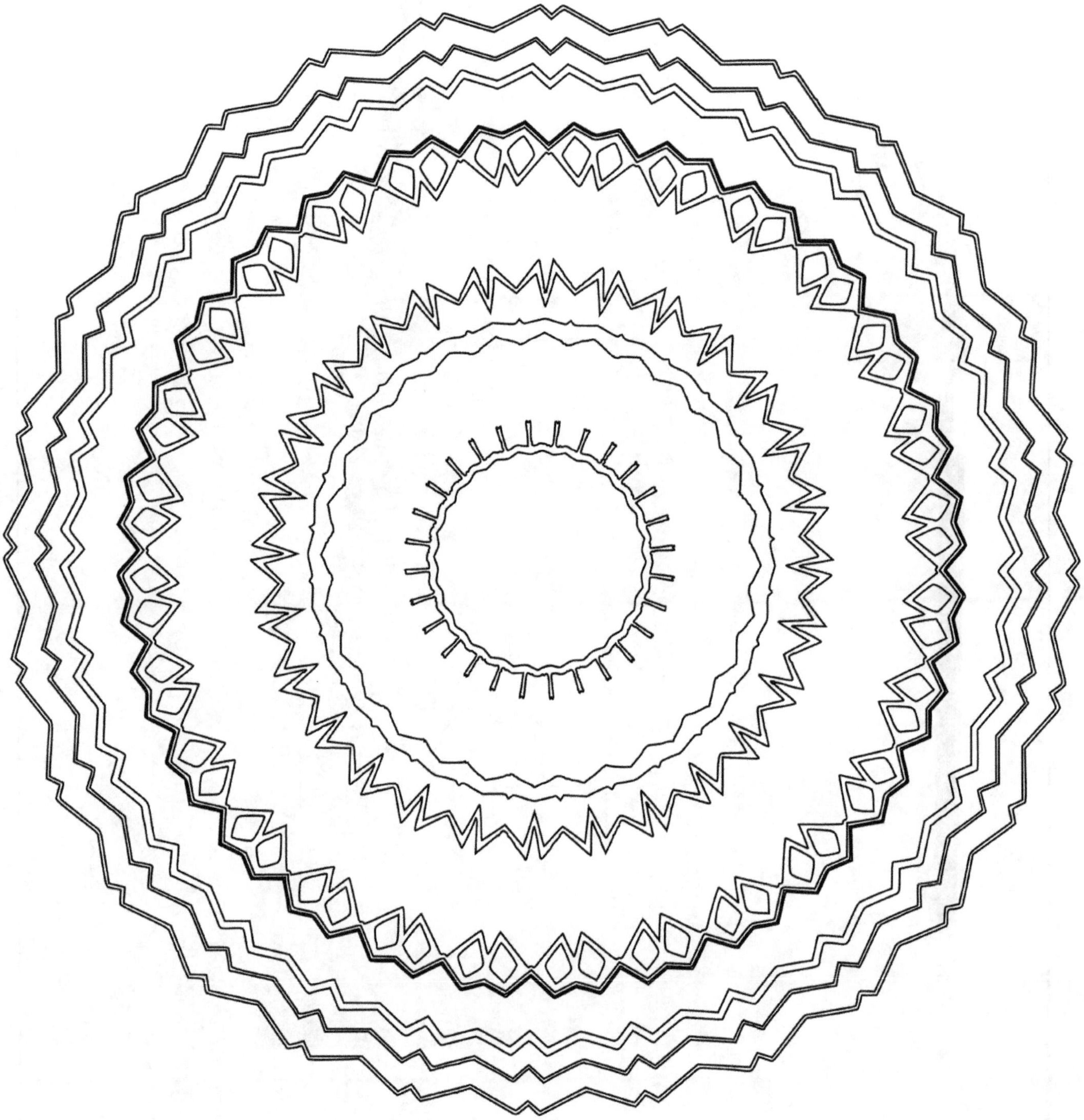

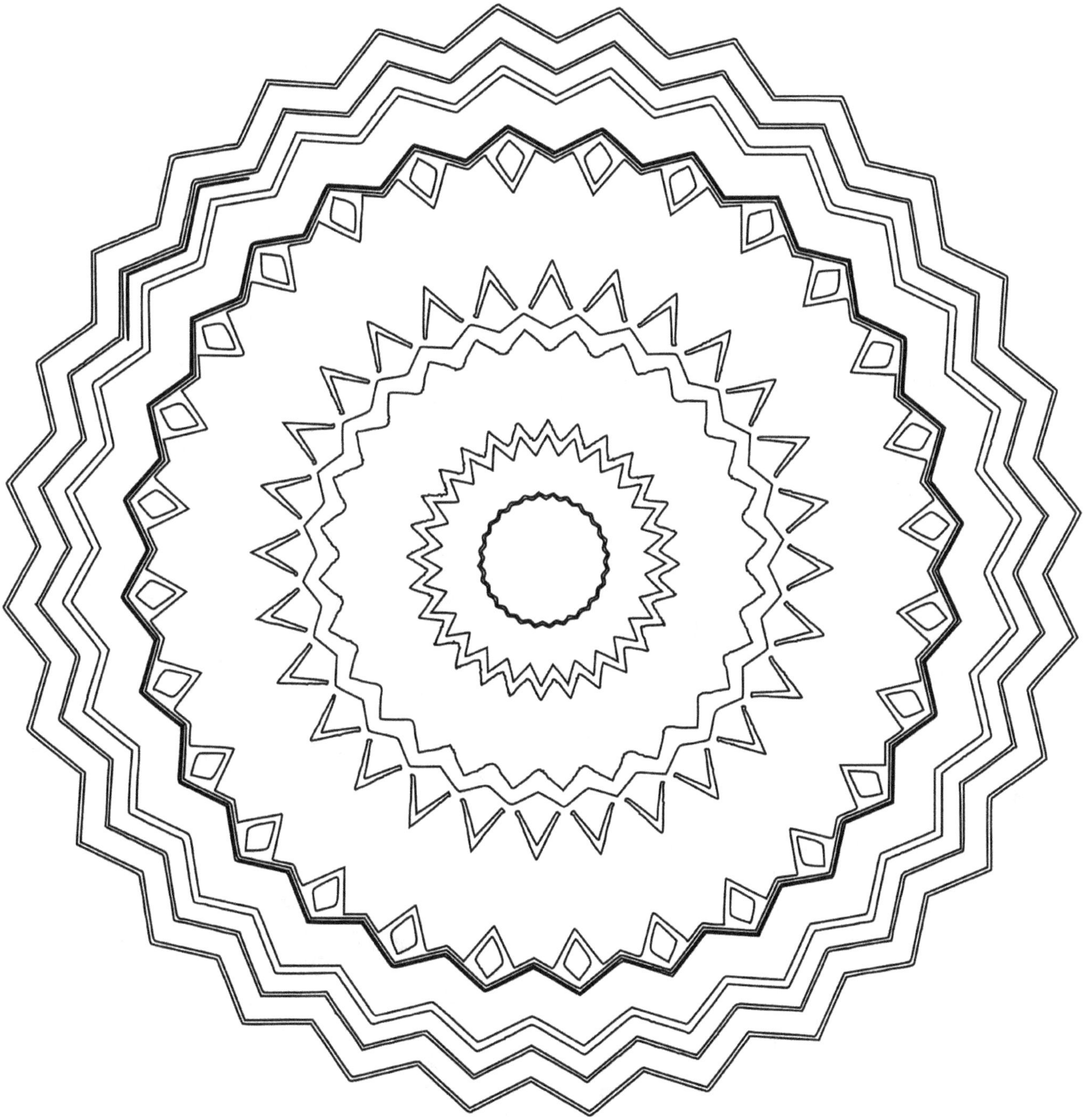

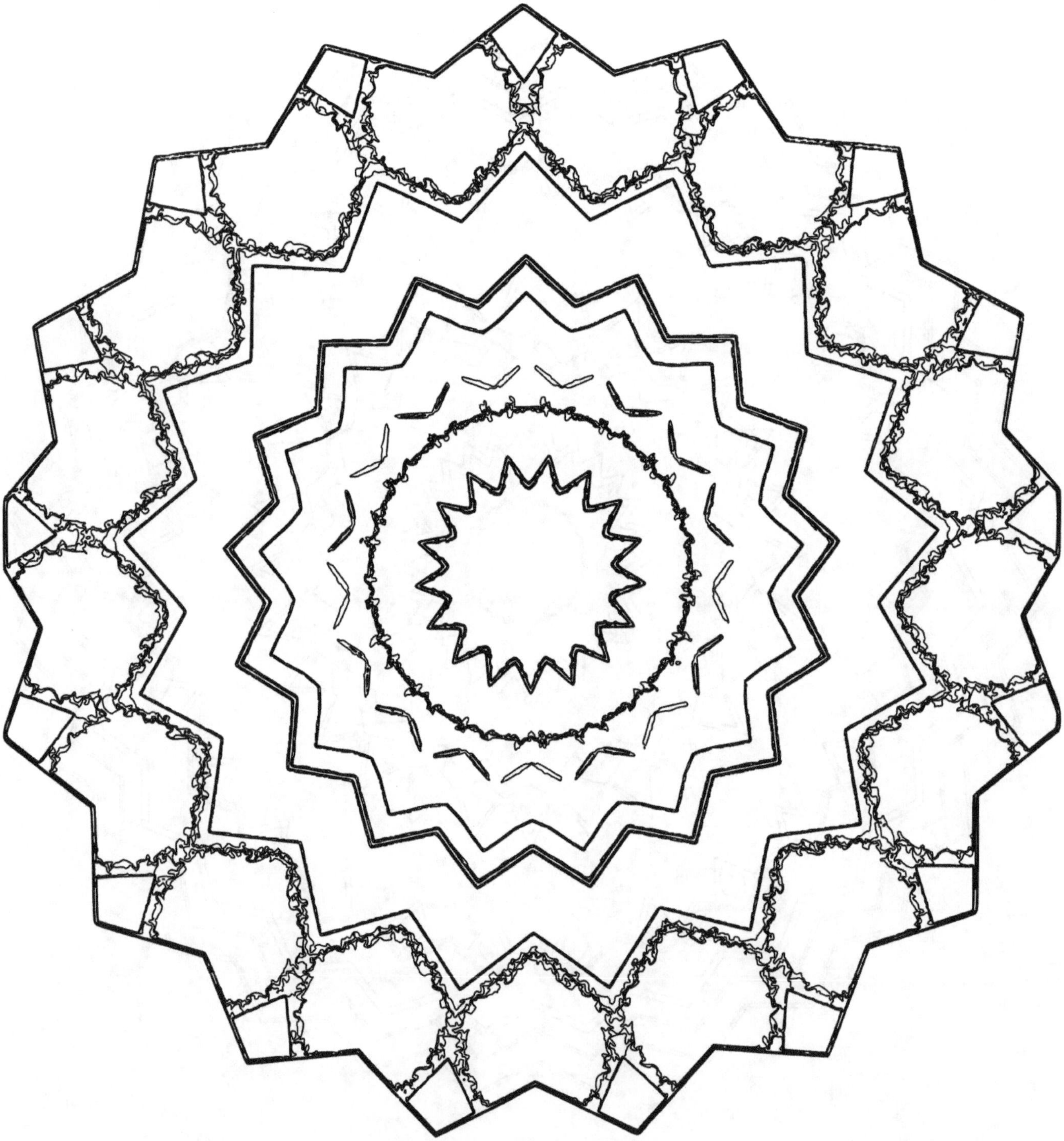

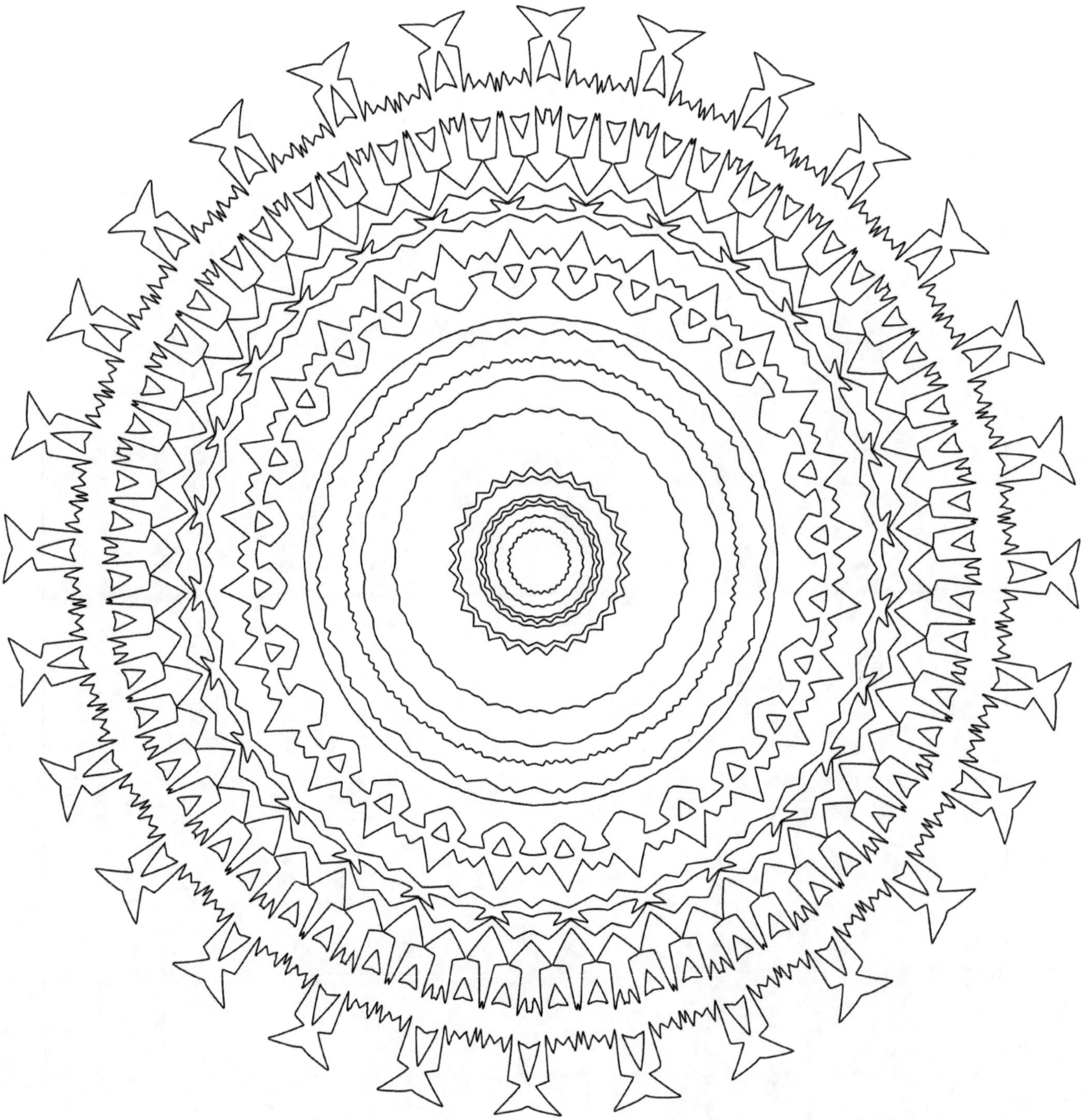

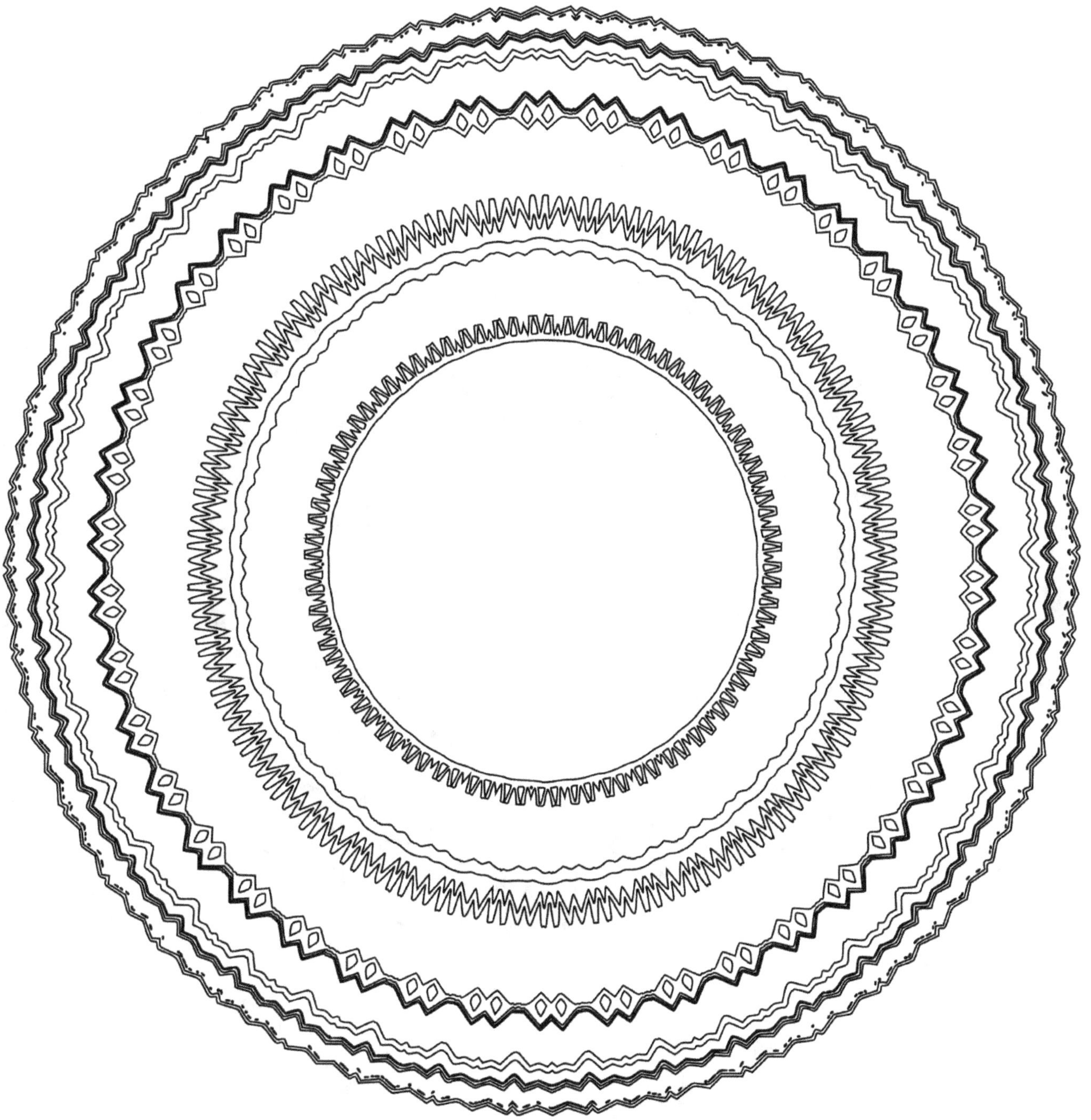

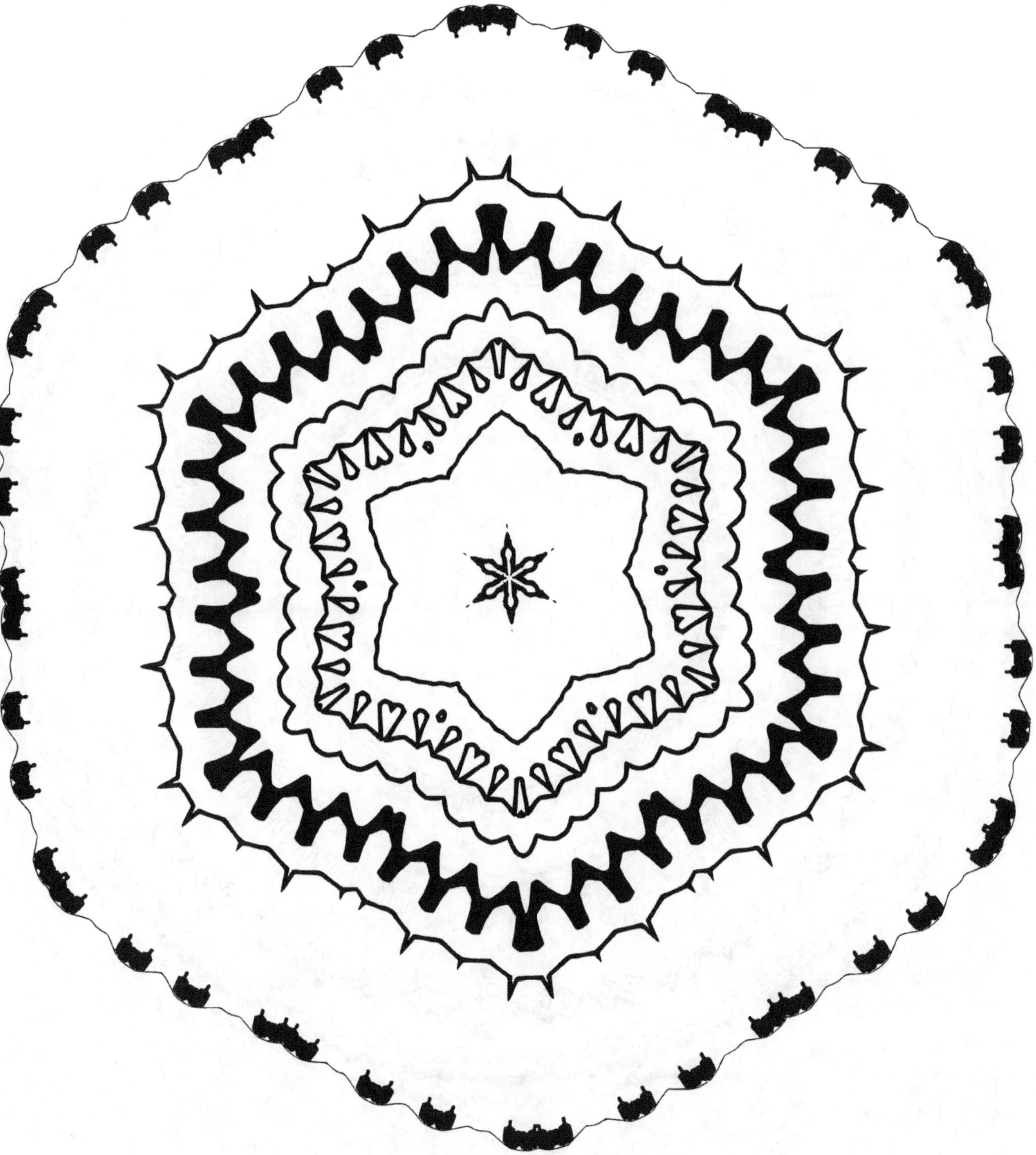

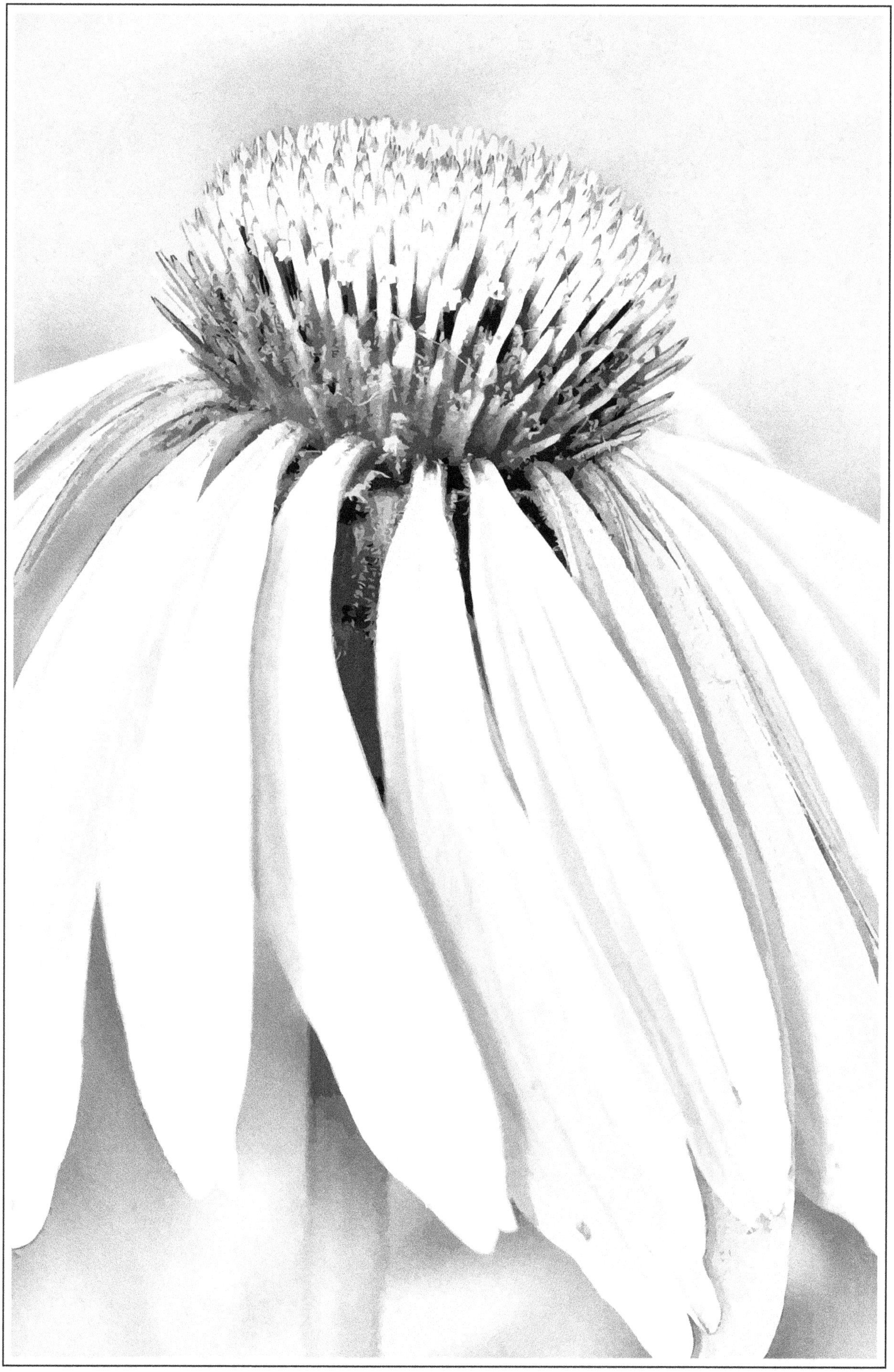

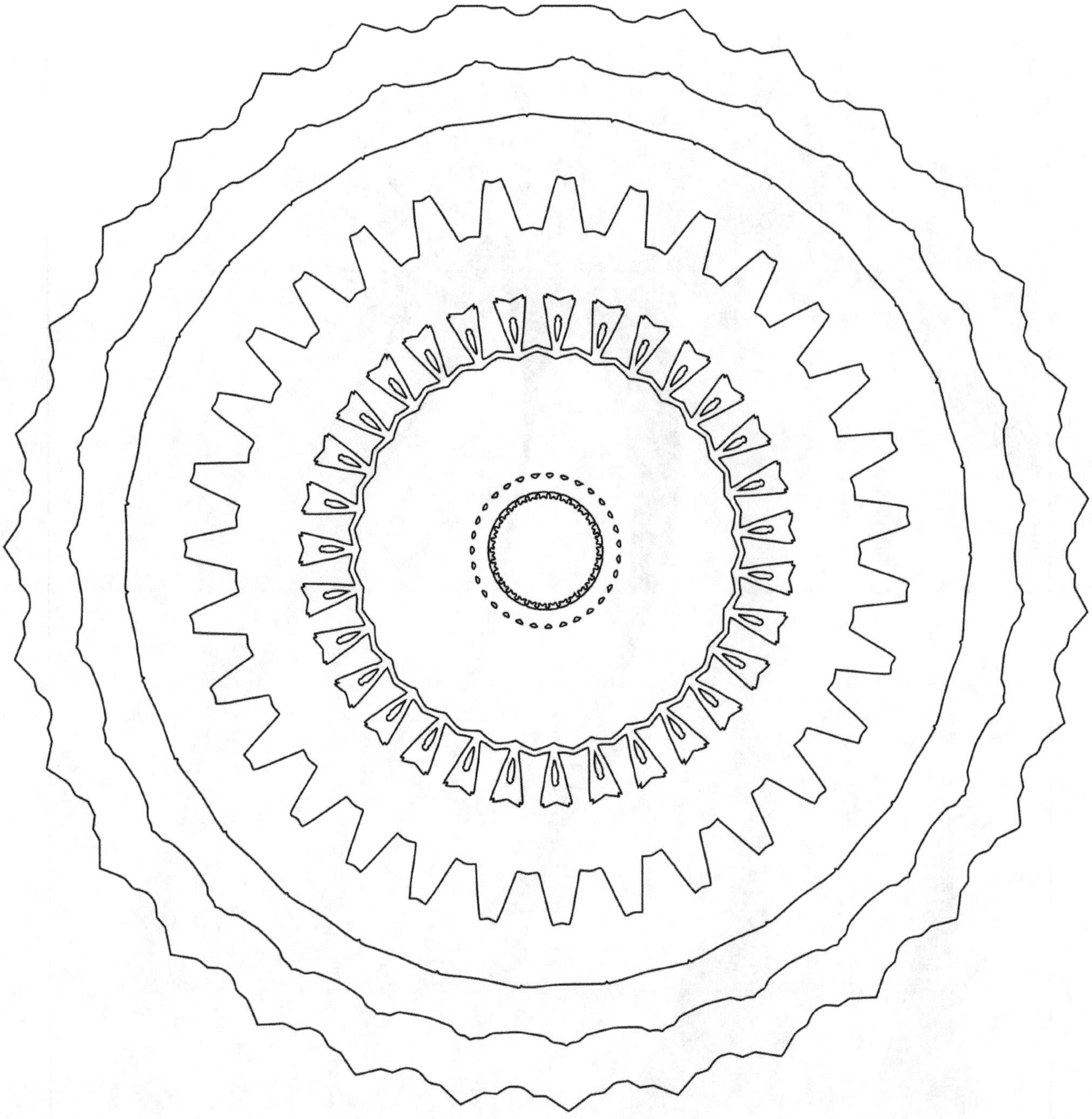

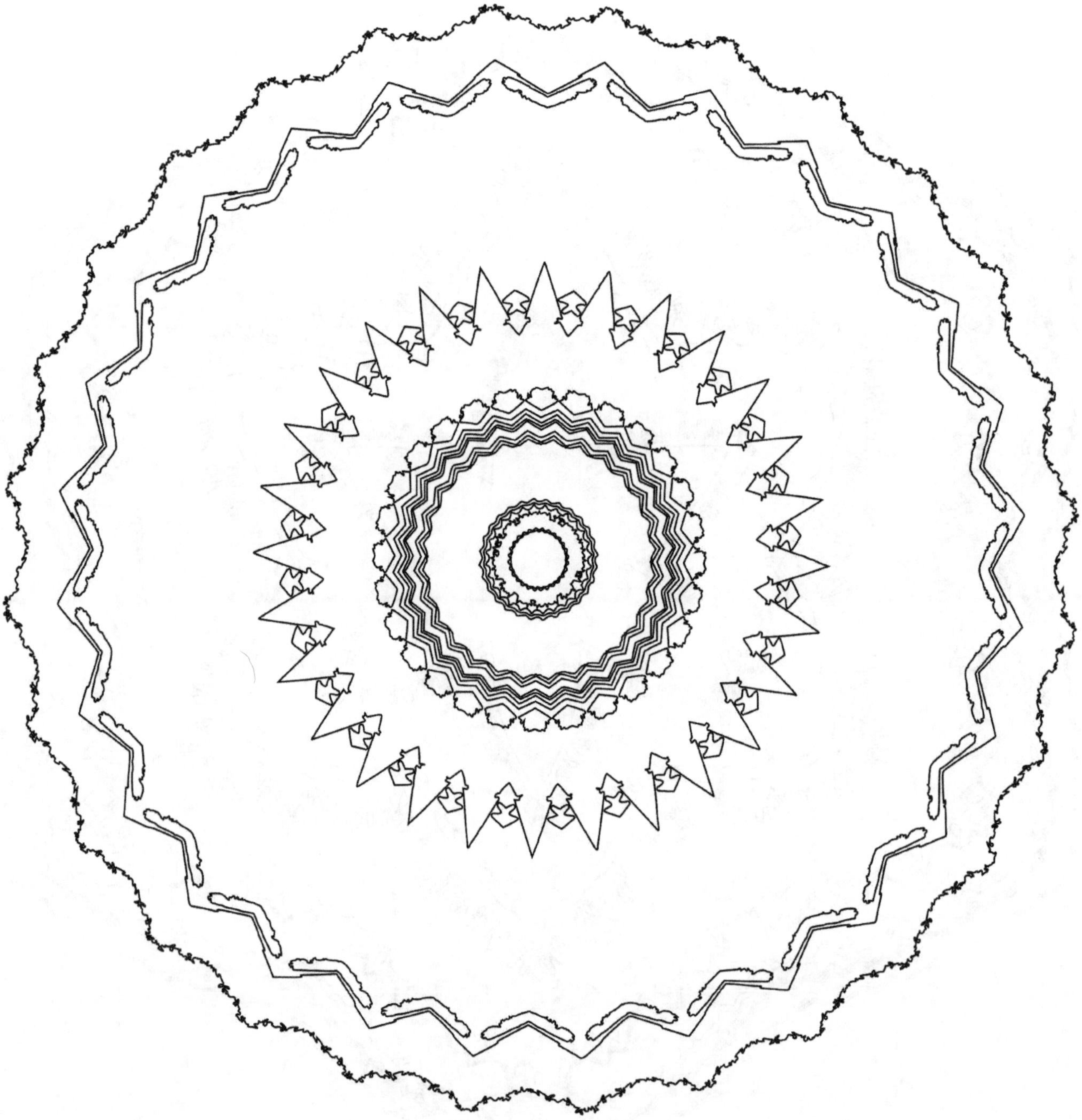

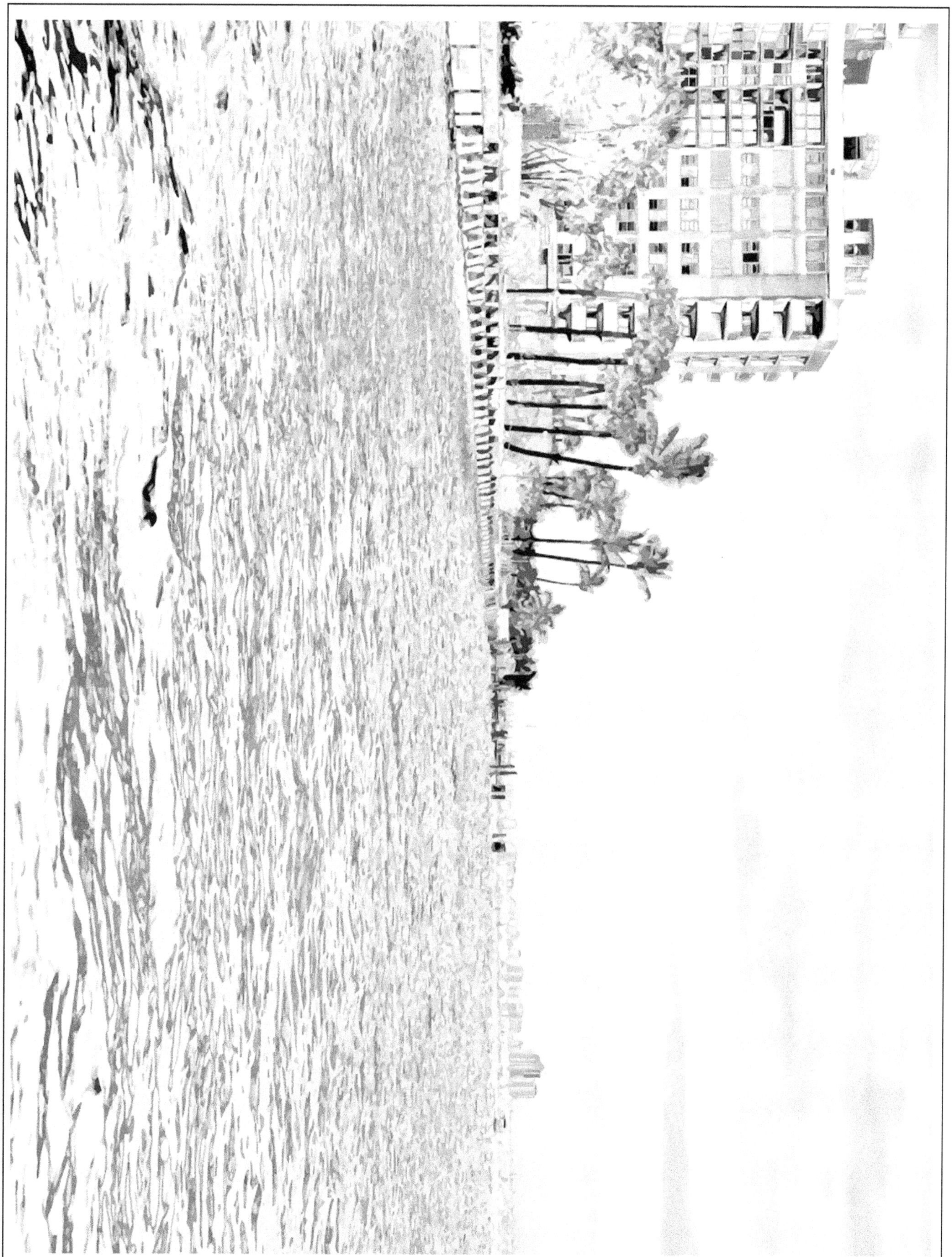

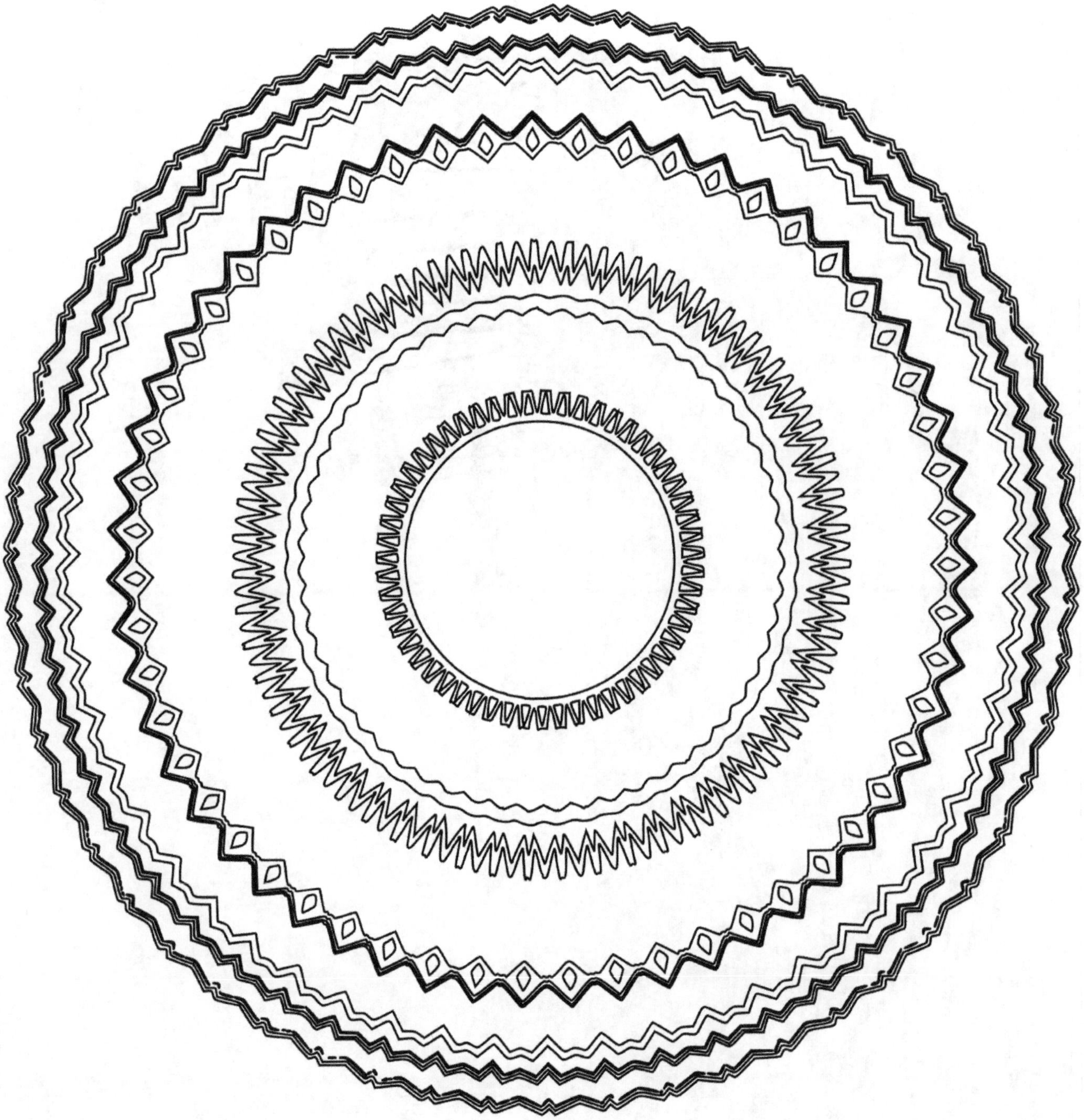

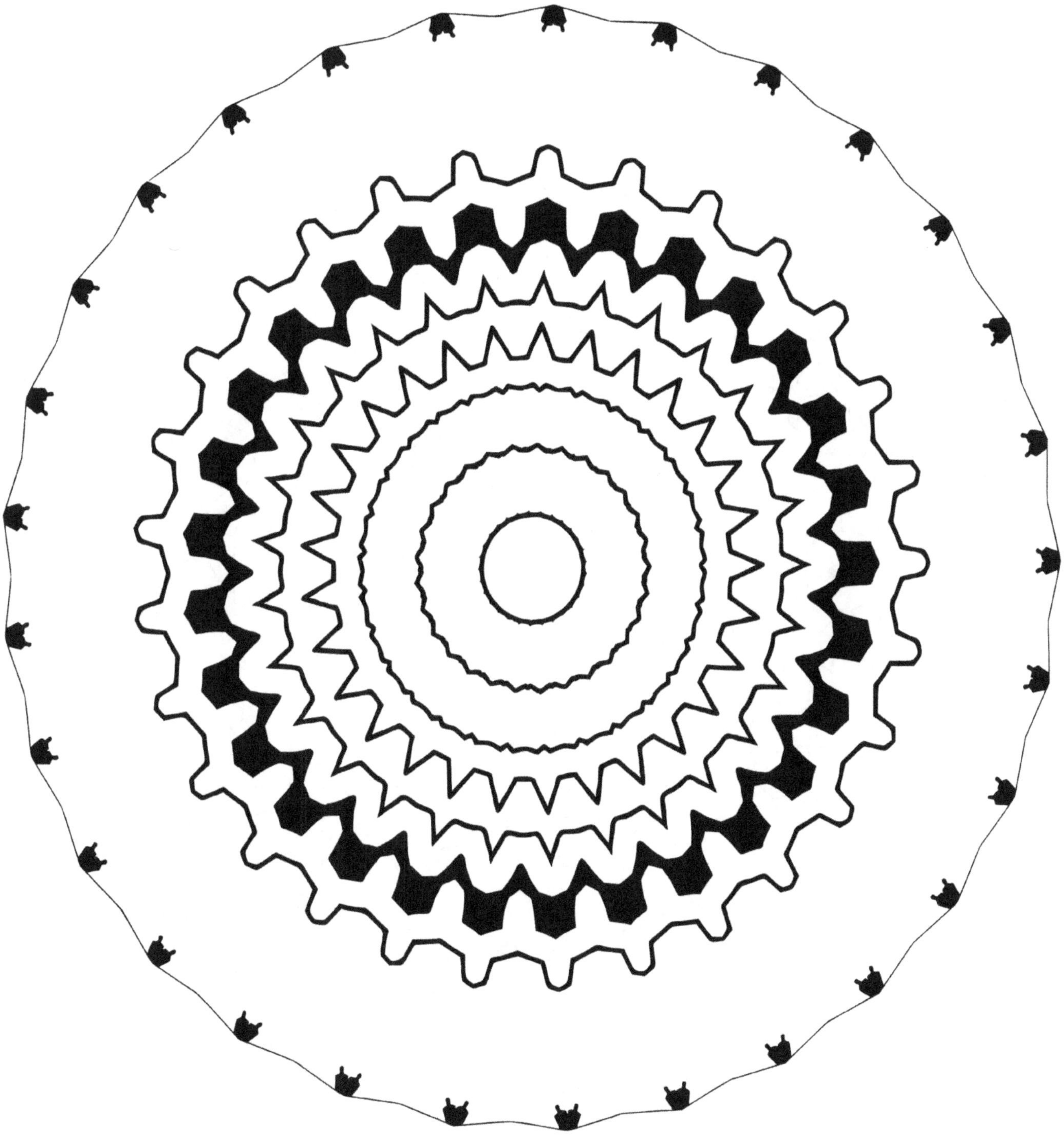

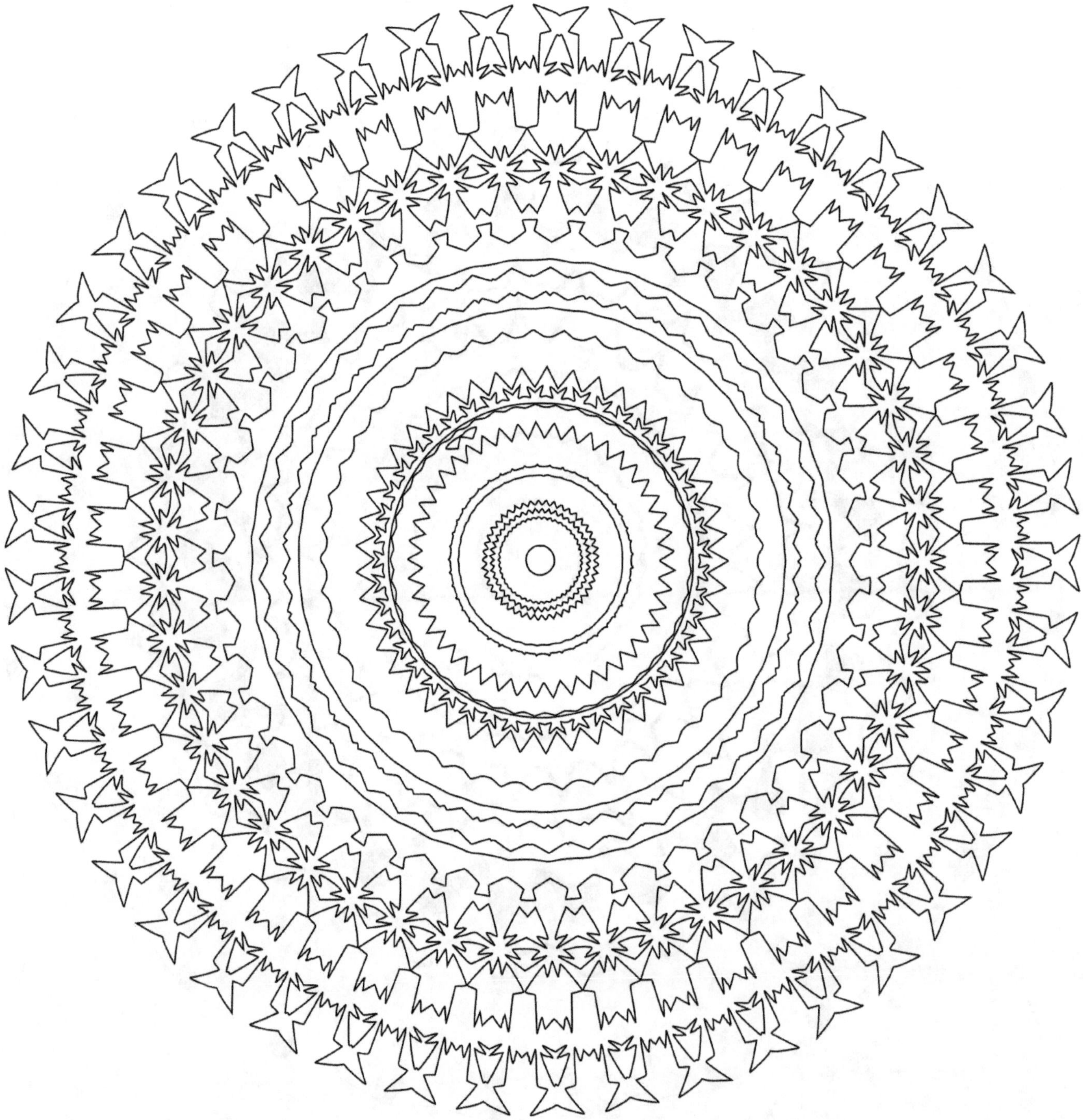

www.ingramcontent.com/pod-product-compliance
Lightning Source LLC
Chambersburg PA
CBHW080625180526
45168CB00007B/3055
* 9 7 8 1 5 1 7 7 6 1 0 2 8 *